First published in 1995 by
Young Library Ltd
The Old Brushworks
Pickwick Road
Corsham
Wiltshire

ISBN 1 85429 023 1

Printed in Hong Kong

Editor: Karen Foster
Designer: Ann Samuel
Consultant: Esmé Daniels, The Board of Deputies of British Jews, London

Artwork on pages 9 and 12-13 by Jeremy Pyke and pages 11, 20, 31, 34, 35, and 39 by Andrew Midgeley.

Picture credits: Chris Lawrence: p.9.27. Behram Kapadia: p.8,14. Hutchinson Library: p.11,17, 18, 19(bottom), 21(both), 24,25,26,28,29,30,31,40,41. Christine Osborne Pictures: p.15(top), 19(top), 23,37,38. Peter Newark Pictures: p.16. Springboard: p.10,15(bottom), 35,36,39.

JEWRY

The customs, culture and religion of
Jews around the world

Clive A Lawton

YOUNG LIBRARY

CONTENTS

WHAT IS JUDAISM?

Judaism is the religion of the Jews. It was started by Abraham, who was the very first Jew. Abraham lived over 3,500 years ago in Iraq, and he believed in one god in a time when people worshipped many gods.

Abraham took his family from Iraq to Israel because he believed that God promised him Israel would belong to him and his descendants for ever. The Israelites then moved to Egypt to escape famine in Israel, and many of them were forced into slavery by the Egyptian king, or Pharoah, as he was called. They were finally rescued by a new leader called Moses who led them out of Egypt and back to their homeland, Israel. This famous escape is called the Exodus.

This ancient manuscript from Sarajevo in the former Yugoslavia tells the story of Moses, who is shown here holding the Ten Commandments.

Moses and the Ten Commandments

Whilst on their journey, in the desert, they stopped at Mount Sinai. It was here that Jews believe God gave Moses ten rules for the Israelites to live by. These were the Ten Commandments, and they were written on two tablets of stone. They became the basis for the Israelites' religious lives, and are all written in the Jewish holy book, which is called the Torah. The Torah consists of the first five books of the Bible. Many other rules for Jewish life are written down in another book called the Talmud.

When they returned to Israel, the Israelites led a happy life under the wise king David and his son

Solomon. Solomon built a huge temple to God in Jerusalem, which is why it is an important city for all Jews. When Solomon died, his kingdom split. The northern tribes were scattered and conquered by the Assyrians. The words Jew and Judaism come from the southern kingdom, Judea.

The Teachings of Judaism

The Torah and the Talmud teach Jews that they should respect all people. They think that God chose them to carry his message. They try to obey the laws of the Torah and do not try to convert other people to become Jews. There is more about this over the page.

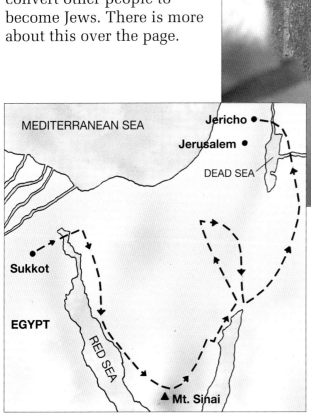

This map shows the journey the Jewish people had to make in Biblical times.

The Western wall, sometimes called the Wailing Wall in Jerusalem is all that is left of the ancient temple. Jews gather here to pray and often write prayers on paper which they put in the cracks between the stones.

WHAT IS A JEW?

Being a Jew means more than just belonging to the Jewish religion. It also means belonging to one very large family.

If you decided you did not want to see any of your family again, you would still be part of the same family. In the same way, if a Jew decided that he no longer believed in God he would still be a Jew. Most Jews celebrate the most important festivals in their tradition, and in this way they feel connected to other Jews all over the world.

A chosen people

The idea that God chose the Jews to spread his message has caused many difficulties for them throughout history. Other people often resented the thought of the Jews' special relationship with God and persecuted the Jewish people.

Jews who settled in some Christian countries were attacked and killed. England, France and other countries drove the Jews out.

People meeting outside the synagogue. Can you see the Star of David on the wall?

But there were exceptions. In the thirteenth century, the Jews were allowed to play a useful part in Spanish life and the country became a great civilisation. Turkey and Poland also welcomed them. Many Jews went to Russia, and by the nineteenth century there were Jews in most European and Asian countries. However, there were many laws against them. They could not mix easily and many were poor.

The worst case of Jews being persecuted was in the Second World War. Adolf Hitler ordered Jews all over Europe to be rounded up into concentration camps, where many died or were

About 2.5 million people were killed at the concentration camp at Auschwitz in Poland.

murdered in terrible conditions. There were 8-9 million Jews in Europe between 1940 and 1945, and in that time, Hitler had about 6 million of them killed. One million were children. This mass murder of Jews is called the Holocaust.

After the Holocaust, Jews all over the world felt defeated and sad. But they also felt even closer to the Jewish family and wanted their own homeland again. This desire is called Zionism, because in the Bible, Zion is a poetic word meaning the land of Israel.

In 1948, part of Palestine was declared the independant state of Israel as a new homeland for the Jews. Many had already moved there in the nineteenth century, and many more have now returned. All Jews, wherever they are, have a special feeling for modern Israel.

Find out more about ...

The Star of David

The Star of David is the symbol most closely associated with the Jewish people, although its exact meaning is unclear. Some people think that it represents the shield used by King David. Others say that its corners show the six working days of the week and its centre the Sabbath, or holy day. The Israeli flag has the Star of David at its centre.

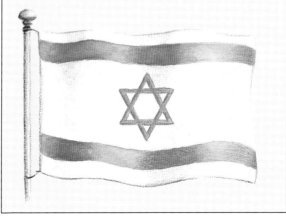

WHERE DO JEWS LIVE?

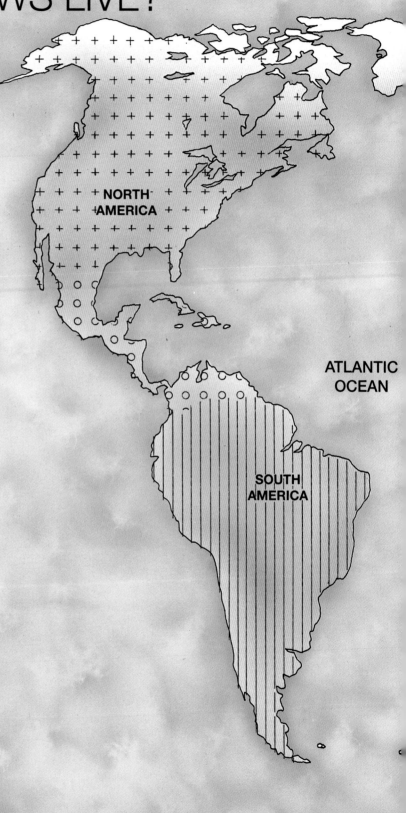

Although Israel is the Jewish homeland, there are Jews in almost every other country, and there are approximately 14 million Jewish people living throughout the world.

This map shows the countries where Jews live and the size of the populations.

NORTH AMERICA

ATLANTIC OCEAN

SOUTH AMERICA

Jewish Population

	less than 5,000
	5,000–50,000
	50,000–250,000
	250,000–1million
	1million–5million
	over 5million

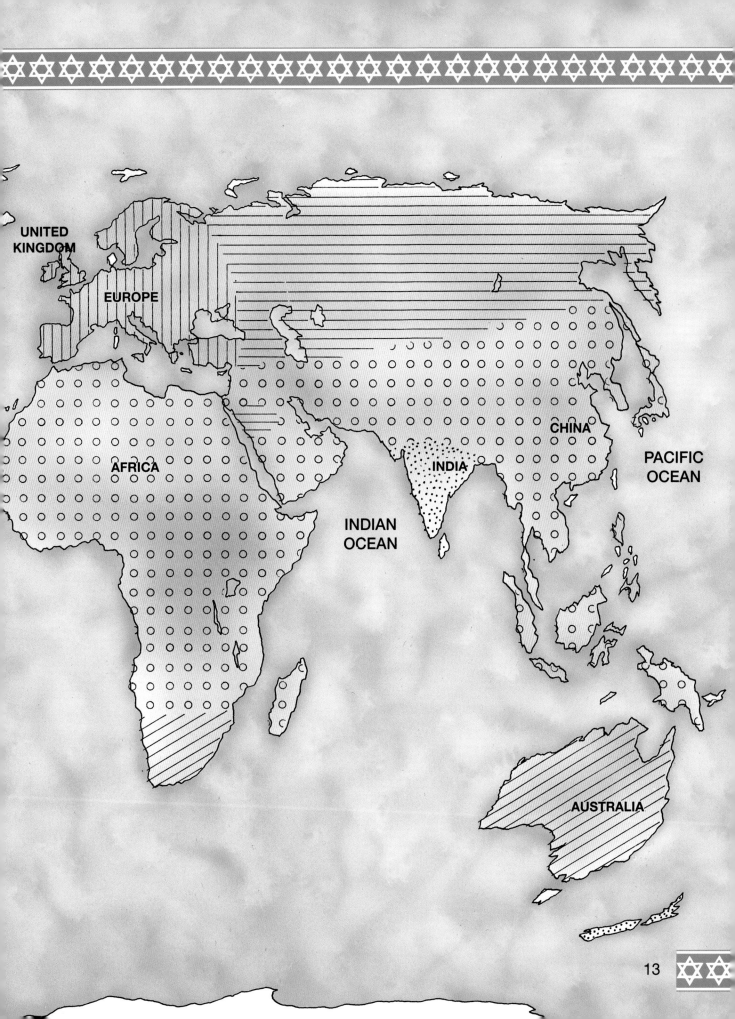

UNITED
KINGDOM

EUROPE

AFRICA

INDIAN
OCEAN

INDIA

CHINA

PACIFIC
OCEAN

AUSTRALIA

13

DIFFERENT KINDS OF JEWS

You know that there are Jews in many countries in the world. They all share a common history and traditions but they are not all the same. An American Jew is very different from an Indian Jew or a Spanish Jew. Even Jews who live in the same country can be different from each other. There are different kinds of Jewish groups.

Ashkenazim or Sephardim?

Jews are divided into two main groups – Ashkenazim and Sephardim. Ashkenazim come from Europe and other western countries, while Sephardim come from Mediterranean and Arabic-speaking countries. While both groups pray in Hebrew, the Jewish language, they pronounce it slightly differently and have other different traditions and forms of prayer.

Orthodox or Reform?

Ashkenazim can be orthodox or reform Jews, depending on how strongly they feel the Torah should be studied and followed. Orthodox Jews take the teachings very seriously indeed. They follow all the rules and traditions of Judaism and pray in Hebrew three times every day - in the morning, afternoon and evening. Men and women always pray separately and an Orthodox Jewish man will usually have his head covered as a sign of respect for God. Reform Jews might be just as religious but they do not follow all the traditional rituals, believing that they are not necessarily the word of God. Men and women will sit together to pray and many prayers are said in the local language.

This picture shows a Hasidic Jewish man from Jerusalem.

Hasidic Jews have long side curls and distinctive clothes.

You can see that these children are Jewish because the boys are wearing skull caps.

Hasidic Jews

Hasidic Jews look very distinctive, with long black coats, long side curls and fur hats, as in the above picture. They follow a mystic and teacher who lived in Eastern Europe in the seventeenth century. They believe in kindness and joyful services including singing and dancing, although they keep to themselves and do not mix much with other Jews. Today the main Hasidic centre is in the city of New York.

Secular Jews

Secular Jews are non-religious Jews. They like to follow the Jewish traditions but do not obey the religious rules. They feel Jewish and have a special relationship with Israel.

WHAT ARE JEWS LIKE?

As with most groups of people, it is very hard to generalise about characteristics of the Jews. Jewish people are just like other people! However, there are certain qualities which most Jews appear to have in common.

From an early age Jews learn to be hardworking. They have extra lessons at the synagogue to learn Hebrew and to find out about their culture and traditions. Their attitude to hard work is clearly seen on the small farming villages called kibbutzim in Israel. Members of a kibbutz have no money of their own. They work together for the good of the small community and in return they get everything they need to live.

Many Jewish people are musical and singing plays a large part in their religious and daily lives. There are many famous Jews in the music world, such as George Gershwin and Irving Berlin, who used Jewish musical traditions to form modern music.

Jews are brought up to have a great respect for families and traditions, with a deep sense of what is right and wrong. Education and helping society are very important and as a result many Jews become lawyers, doctors and politicians. One very famous Jewish politician, Benjamin Disraeli, was made British Prime Minister in 1868 and is considered to be the founder of the Conservative Party.

Everyone works together on a kibbutz in Israel. Here it is harvest time.

This is the cover of a musical score by the American composer Irving Berlin.

JEWISH CLOTHES

Although most Jews tend to wear ordinary clothes according to the country they live in, there are several items of traditional dress. These are worn for festivals or for praying at the synagogue.

Jews believe that it is a sign of respect to God to cover your head, especially when praying. You may have seen some Jewish men wearing a kipah, which is a small cap which sits on the back of the head. Orthodox men wear a kipah every day. Orthodox married women cover their heads with a beautiful scarf. This is particularly worn when the candles are lit at the beginning of Shabbat.

Clothes for religious services

Jewish men wear a prayer cloak called a tallit in the synagogue. It is white with black or coloured stripes. At each corner is a long tassel knotted in a special way to remember the laws of the Torah. For special occasions they may also wear a white robe called a kitel. The kitel represents the dress of the ancient priests.

On weekdays, men also wear two small black leather boxes called tefillin which, in Hebrew, means 'prayer object'. The tefillin shel rosh is worn on the forehead and the tefillin shel yad on the upper arm. Both are worn during morning prayer attached with leather straps. Inside each box are passages from the Torah written on small scrolls of parchment.

Jewish boys are taught how to strap on the tefillin.

The prayer cloak, or tallit, is worn around the shoulders throughout prayers.

Long, black coats are the most distinctive part of Hasidic Jewish costume.

Hasidic costume

You read about Hasidic Jews on page 15. They have a distinctive set of clothes. The men wear a velvet kipah under a black, wide-brimmed hat called a shtreimel and long black coats. They also wear their hair in long curls over their ears because the Torah says that Jews must not cut the corners of their hair.

19

JEWISH LANGUAGES

Shalom readers!

The greeting used among Jewish people is the Hebrew word, Shalom, which means peace. Hebrew is the language used by the Jews and is one of the oldest living languages in the world. The Torah and the Talmud were written in Hebrew but for well over 1,000 years hardly anyone spoke Hebrew. Then in the 1900s, Hebrew was revived with the growth of Zionism, and is today the language of the state of Israel. No matter what language they normally speak, Jews pray in Hebrew. This means that Jewish children have to go to special classes, sometimes as many as three times a week, and learn a new language so that they can pray.

The Hebrew alphabet is written on this page. There are 22 letters. Vowels are not normally used once the language has been learnt. Hebrew is read from right to left across the page.

Vowels

When vowels are used, they are dots or dashes added to letters as below.

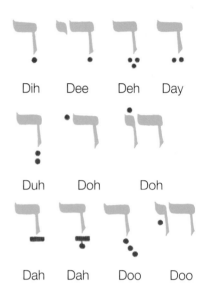

Dih	Dee	Deh	Day
Duh	Doh	Doh	
Dah	Dah	Doo	Doo

Consonants

| Khaph | Kaph | Yod | Tet | Het | Zayin | Vav | Ho | Dalet | Gimel | Vet | Bet | Aleph |

| Tav | Sin | Shin | Resh | Koph | Tsadi | Feh | Peh | Ayin | Samekh | Nun | Mem | Lamed |

Yiddish

Yiddish is another Jewish language. It was the language developed by Central and Eastern European Jews hundreds of years ago and is mainly German with some Hebrew added. The name Yiddish comes from the German word for Jewish which is Judisch. Yiddish is always changing. Although written in the Hebrew alphabet it is always borrowing words from other languages.

This Jewish boy is learning Hebrew. If you look carefully, you will see the Hebrew word for 'pencil' written on the blackboard.

Find out more about......

Hebrew

Here is the Hebrew word 'Shadai', meaning 'Almighty'. written on a special Jewish box called a mezuzah. The boxes are attached to the right side of every doorpost in the house. They contain a prayer from the Torah. Some people touch the mezuzah on the front door of the house as they go in and out.

Mezuzot like this are a common sight in Jewish households

JEWISH FOOD

In the Torah there are rules which govern how Jews eat. They are required to eat kosher food. Kosher is a Hebrew word which means correct and only foods which fit the rules in the Torah can be called kosher. This means that Jews have to be careful about the foods they buy. For example, bread can only be labelled kosher if it has not been prepared on Shabbat, and contains no forbidden fat.

Eating meat

The Torah says that only animals that chew the cud and have cloven hooves can be eaten. This means that Jews can eat meat from cows and sheep, but not from pigs. And the meat they can eat must be prepared in a certain way, called shehitah. There is more about this at the end of the page.

Fish can be eaten, but only if it has had scales and fins. This means that shellfish is not allowed.

Eating at home

Orthodox Jews do not mix milk and meat foods. So they cannot put butter on a beef sandwich or drink white coffee with it. Kosher homes have one set of dishes and cooking utensils for preparing and cooking meat and a completely different set for preparing dairy products. You can see that it is not easy to follow the kosher laws, and special effort has to be made.

The labels on all the foods show that they are kosher.

 Find out more about...

Shehitah

Shehitah is the name given to the slaughter of animals for kosher food. It must be carried out by a special butcher who says a blessing while he kills the animal. He does it as quickly as he can to cause the animal as little pain as possible. Before the meat is cooked it is soaked in cold water and then covered with salt to drain it of as much blood as possible.

Salt beef is a favourite Jewish food. Here it is being carved.

A PLACE TO PRAY

Look out for the Ner Tamid and the replicas of the stone tablets inside the synagogue in this picture.

Jews worship in a special building called a synagogue. Synagogues are usually quite large, because they are also a centre for education and social life in the community. From the outside they may not look like a place of worship, although if you look closely you might see a Star of David or some words of Hebrew on the building. There may be a hall attached where adults and children are taught Hebrew, Jewish history and religion. The hall is also used to hold parties for celebrations such as weddings.

Inside the synagogue

How a synagogue is decorated depends on the country it is in. It may be plain and bare with wooden seats and white walls. Or it may be quite elaborate with brass lamps and red velvet seats. But there are always certain things to look out for.

The Ark

The Ark is a cupboard where the richly decorated scrolls of Torah are kept. When the scrolls are not in use, a curtain called a

parokhet is drawn across it. It is the most important place in the synagogue, and is found against the wall that faces Jerusalem. Over the Ark are replicas of the two stone tablets, where the first two words of each of the Ten Commandments are written, as well as the inscription 'Know before whom you stand'. There is a picture of the Tablets on page 8.

The Ner Tamid

Near the Ark is the Ner Tamid – the everlasting light. It is usually a decorative electric lamp which is switched on all the time, reminding worshippers that God is always present. You may see a seven-branched candlestick, called the Menorah. This is the light described to the Jews by God in the desert. Its function is now performed by the Ner Tamid.

The service is led from the Bimah.

The Bimah

There is a raised platform in the centre of the synagogue from which all services are led. At each morning service there is a reading from the scrolls of Torah, until the whole of the Torah has been read, which takes one year. Prayers are also chanted by a cantor who has a special knowledge of traditional music. Services are held three times a day. Elders of the synagogue, who are honoured men in the community sit in front of the Bimah. Men and women sit separately. In Reform synagogues, where services are held on Shabbat and festivals, men and women sit together.

You can....

Visit a synagogue

Ask your parents or teacher to help you find out exactly what a synagogue looks like by visiting one in your area. Look out for the special features you have read about. Perhaps you know a Jew who could tell you about what the synagogue means to Jewish people.

THE TORAH

The scroll of Torah, or Sefer Torah in Hebrew, which is kept inside the Ark in the synagogue is the most important item in Jewish religious services. Each time it is used there is a ceremonial opening of the Ark. The curtain is drawn aside and the congregation stand and sing as a scroll is removed. This ceremony is called Petikhah.

The words of the Torah are written by a trained scribe on strips of parchment using a quill pen. The strips are sewn together to form a long roll and each end is bound to a wooden rod. The scrolls are then enclosed in wooden or velvet cases which are often beautifully decorated.

Jewish teaching says that every Jew has a duty to write a Torah scroll. In practice this often means contributing money towards the cost of a scroll for the local synagogue.

A scroll of Torah rolls up onto two wooden rods.

The writing of the last few words of a Torah scroll is usually an occasion for celebration.

On the ninth day of the Sukkot festival there is a thanksgiving ceremony called Simkhat Torah, which in Hebrew means 'celebrating the Torah'. The scrolls are paraded seven times round the Bimah in the synagogue while the congregation sing and dance.

Find out more about....

The rabbi

Rabbi is a Hebrew word meaning 'my master' or 'my teacher'. Each synagogue is led by a rabbi who conducts services and teaches others about the Jewish religion. The rabbi is an important person in the Jewish community. He not only takes part in their religious lives but also gives help and advice in everyday matters. Training to become a rabbi takes many years of study at a college called a yeshiva. In Reform synagogues, women can now become rabbis.

The rabbi helps Jewish children to learn about their religion.

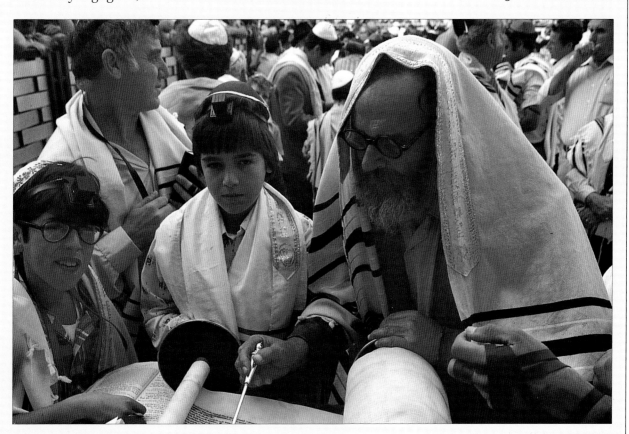

JEWISH TRADITIONS

Like other religions, Judaism has special ceremonies to mark important occasions like the birth of a child, coming of age, marriage and death.

When a child is born

Every child born to a Jewish mother is a Jew, and remains a Jew no matter what happens when he or she grows up. Each Jewish baby is given a Hebrew name, usually in memory of a relative, which is used on special occasions in the synagogue.

Growing up

At 13 years of age, a Jewish boy officially becomes an adult. He has studied for about a year and learnt to sing from the Torah before the ceremony which is called his Barmitzvah. In Hebrew Barmitzvah means 'Son of the Commandment'. At the ceremony in the synagogue he reads from the Torah scroll for the first time in public to show that he is now part of the adult community. A Batmitzvah – 'daughter of the Commandment' – takes place for girls at the age of 12. These occasions usually deserve a party!

This boy reads from the Torah at a practice for his Barmitzvah.

Marriage

A Jewish wedding can take place anywhere. Many marry in the synagogue, but it can be in the open air or in a hotel. It doesn't matter where it is as long as the ceremony takes place under a special canopy called a

huppa. The huppa represents the home that the man and woman will make together. The bride and groom exchange a legal contract called a ketuba which puts in writing the responsibilities that a man has towards his wife. Reform Jews also include the responsibilities that a woman has towards her husband. Traditional Jewish dancing often takes place at weddings.

A Jewish couple are married under a huppa.

When people die

When a Jewish person dies, the body is washed and dressed in simple linen covers. Orthodox Jews do not employ anyone to do this – it falls to people in the community who volunteer to help. The funeral is held as soon as possible so that the community can then get on supporting the dead person's family.

The immediate family will spend a week at home, mourning and being comforted by family and friends. This week is called Shiva, which means 'seven'. Another meaning is 'sitting' which refers to the time they spend sitting on low chairs which show how low they feel because of their loss. Mourners also wear a piece of torn clothing because in the Bible people would tear their clothes to show how sad they were. At the end of the week the family are able to face the world. Every year on the anniversary of the death the family will light a candle at home and say a prayer in the synagogue to remember the person who has died.

SHABBAT

Shabbat, or Sabbath, is the day of the week when Jews rest, celebrate and worship. It starts at sunset on Friday and finishes at nightfall on Saturday. Many Jewish shops and offices are shut. Orthodox Jews will not travel, go shopping or work. Jews spend Shabbat with their families and at the synagogue.

Shabbat begins with a family meal. The woman of the household lights two candles to brighten the special day, and then covers her eyes while she says a blessing. The meal begins with the father making a blessing, called kiddush, over a cup of wine which is shared by everyone. He then says another blessing over two loaves of white bread called challot. All meals eaten on Shabbat are joyous occasions.

Shabbat songs, or Zemirot in Hebrew, are sung at the table to praise God and add to the happy atmosphere. Although most of the songs are learned off by heart, there are booklets containing songs for singing at different times during Shabbat.

Cutting the challot.

Two candles are lit at the start of the Shabbat meal.

 Find out more about ...

The end of Shabbat

At the end of Shabbat there is a small ceremony to mark the end of the day. A plaited candle is lit and sweet spices are smelt while a cup of wine is filled to overflowing. This symbolises the joy of Shabbat spilling over into the next week. The ceremony is called Havdallah.

The Havdallah candle, spice box and cup of wine.

Month
Ab (July-Aug) 30 days

Festival
Tisha b'Av (Fast of Av). 1 day long. A 25 hour fast to mourn the destruction of the Temple in Jerusalem.

Month
Elul (Aug-Sept) 29 days

Month
Tamuz (June-July) 29 days

THE JEWISH CALENDAR

The Jewish New Year is in the autumn and there are normally 12 months in the year. Months have either 29 or 30 days each year. Look below to see the names of the months in Hebrew and their usual lengths.

Month
Sivan (May-June) 30 days

Festival
Shavuot (Feast of Weeks). 1-2 days long. Celebrates the giving of the Torah Mount Sinai.

Month
Iyar (April-May) 29 days

Festival
Yom H'atzmaut (Israel's Independence Day). 1 day long.

Month
Nisan (March-April) 30 days

Festival
Pesach (Passover). 7-8 days long. Celebrates the Jews' escape from slavery over 3,500 years ago and the journey back to Israel.

Month
Tishri (Sept-Oct) 30 days

Festival
Rosh Hashana (New Year)
2 days long.
Yom Kippur (Day of Atonement)
Sukkot (Autumn Festival)
7 or 8 days long.

Month
Heshvan (Oct-Nov)
29 days

Month
Kislev (Nov-Dec)
29 or 30 days

Festival
Hannukka (Festival of Lights).
8 days. Celebrates the
rededication of the Temple
in Jerusalem.

You will also find the names of the most important events in the Jewish calendar. These are Holy Days, such as Yom Kippur in the month of Tishri – a day of fasting and prayer when Jews repent of their sins – and festivals. You can read more about some of the festivals later in the book.

Month
Tevet (Dec-Jan) 29 days

Month
Adar (Feb-March) 29 days

Festival
Purim (Feast of Lots). 1 day long. The carnival festival. Celebrates Esther's story in the Bible.

Month
Shevat (Jan-Feb) 30 days

Festival
Tu b'Shevat (New Year for Trees). 1 day. Trees are planted.

33

PASSOVER

The festival of Passover, or Pesach in Hebrew, commemorates the Jews' Exodus from Egypt, which you read about on page 8. It is one of the most popular festivals among Jews.

Before the Passover festival, Jewish families clean their houses from top to bottom to make sure that any forbidden leavened, or risen, food is removed. Then on the first two nights, families gather together to retell the story of the escape from Egypt. Everyone present has a copy of a book called the Haggadah, so that they can follow the story.

The family meal is called the Seder, and special symbolic foods are placed in the centre of the table. Each food tells part of the story. There is unleavened, or unrisen bread called matza. This reminds the Jews that they were in such a hurry to get away from Egypt that they didn't have time to add yeast to the bread for the journey. There is lettuce to remind the family of spring. Bitter herbs bring tears to the eyes and represent the sorrow of slavery in Egypt. Salt water represents the tears cried by the Israelites. A sweet paste of nuts, apple, wine and cinnamon is a reminder of the mortar the Israelites used to cement their bricks together. A roasted bone represents the sacrifice of a lamb on the evening before the Exodus.

By preparing all these foods, Jews bring the Exodus alive each year.

This family are celebrating Passover together

You can see all the Seder foods here.

You can....

Make your own matza

1 Slowly add cold water to 2 cups of plain flour until you have a stiff dough.

2 Roll out the dough until it is very thin - about 3mm - then mark it into squares about 20cm x 20cm.

3 Prick the squares all over with a fork and bake in a hot oven for about 15 minutes.

SUKKOT

When the Jews escaped from Egypt they wandered through the desert for forty years, living in tents. To remember the journey of their ancestors, Jews celebrate the festival of Sukkot for a week each autumn by building a special shelter in which they eat all their meals. The shelter is called a Sukka, and it must have at least three walls and a roof of branches or leaves.

Some families build their own Sukka, by taking the roof from a garden shed and using branches instead. Others use the large Sukka which is built in the grounds of the synagogue. In Israel, many flats are built with balconies suitable for adaptation as a Sukka.

Sukkot is a joyous festival, so that if it rains or is cold, Jews do not have to use their Sukka. If it is warm, however, some families even sleep in their Sukka.

These Hasidic Jews are gathering branches to make the roof of their Sukka.

This family is building a Sukka from their garden shed.

HANNUKKA

More than 2,000 years ago in Israel the Syrians wanted to stop the Jews from practising their religion. After years of fighting, the tiny Jewish army finally defeated the many Syrians. The Jews returned to the Temple and found it in a terrible state. They wanted to light the Menorah, but only found enough holy oil to last for one day. But a miracle happened – the oil lasted for eight days, until a new supply could be made. The winter festival of light, called Hannukka, celebrates this miracle.

Nowadays, Jewish households have a special candlestick with eight branches called a Hanukiya, which is a symbol of the oil lamp in the Temple. One candle is lit every night for the eight nights of Hannukka, until they are all alight. In Jerusalem huge Hanukiyot are placed on top of buildings all over the city, lit with electric light. They are quite a sight!

During Hannukka many families give children small presents each day. They also eat fried food like doughnuts and potato cakes, called latkes. The oil these foods are fried in reminds everyone of the miracle of the oil.

Fried potato cakes, or latkes, are often eaten at Hannukka.

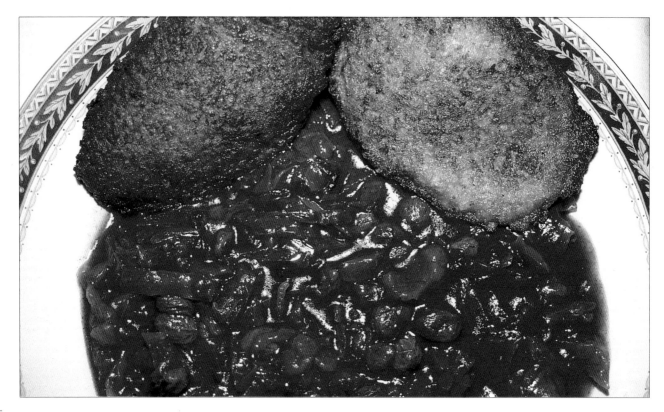

Lighting a hanukiya at home.

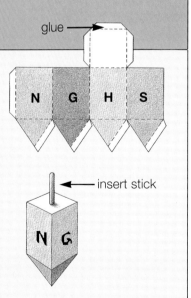

glue →

insert stick

Play the Dreidle game

Jewish children play the Dreidle game at Hannukka. To play you will need to make a dreidle, or spinning top, from card and put a stick through the middle. Look at the pictures to see how to make one yourself. Now mark each side with the first letter of each word of the Hebrew phrase – 'Ness Gadol Haya Sham' – which means ' A great miracle happened there'. Before the game begins, each player puts an agreed number of counters into the kitty. Depending on which letter the dreidle falls on, the spinner takes from or puts into the kitty. This is what each letter means: N = nothing, G = takes all, H = takes half and S = pays into the kitty. Good luck!

THE JEWISH WORLD

This book has given you a lot of information about Judaism and the Jewish people. Now that you are more aware of their culture and religion, you will probably notice much more about Jewish life as it goes on around you.

Jewish people

Look out for Jewish people in the place where you live. You know that it is easy to notice Hasidic Jews as you pass them in the street, because of their distinctive dress. But you might not notice an Orthodox or Reform Jew if you saw one – they may look just like everyone else going by! But they will almost certainly be living a different kind of life to you – think about how Jewish people are celebrating Shabbat while you are shopping on Saturday, for example.

An orthodox Jewish couple chat together in London.

40

The Jewish community

In some cities, like London and Paris, there are areas where many Jews choose to live close to each other. These communities are good places to find Jewish shops and restaurants, where you can try Jewish specialities like latkes or salt beef. You may also be able to find a synagogue open to visitors so that you can see all the special items you read about on pages 24 and 25.

Jewish life

If you have any Jewish friends, you may already have been involved in parts of their lives. You may have taken part in a Passover meal, or danced at a Jewish wedding like the one in this picture. You will feel that you are starting to know about Jewish life, because the best way to really learn about Jewish culture is to experience it for yourself.

Dancing at a traditional Jewish wedding.

QUIZ

Here are some puzzles and questions to test your knowledge of Judaism and the Jews. All the solutions can be found somewhere in this book. When you've finished, look at the answers at the bottom of the page and see how well you've done. Remember not to mark the book.

1 What is the name given to the prayer cloak worn by Jewish men?

2 Unscramble these letters to find the name of a Jewish group: H S E M D P R I A.

3 Which two types of foods do Jewish people never mix?

4 At what age does a Jewish boy officially become an adult?

5 What is a symbol of Jewish culture?

6 Name the city shown on this map detail.

7 What does the Hebrew word 'Shadai' mean?

8 How many letters are there in the Hebrew alphabet?

9 Does Sukkot fall in Spring or Autumn?

10 What does the symbol on this food label mean?

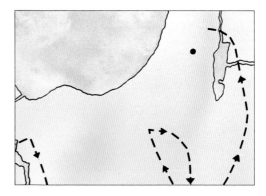

11 Of which ancient building is the Western Wall the only remaining part?

12 Why do the Jews eat unleavened bread at Passover?

13 Fill in the empty spaces to find the name of the Jewish place of worship: S – – A – O G – – .

14 What is the Hebrew word for peace?

15 Orthodox Jewish men and women always pray together. True or false?

16 In what year did Palestine become the independent state of Israel?

17 Name the canopy used for Jewish marriages.

18 What is the name of the ceremony which takes place at the end of the Shabbat in Jewish households?

19 Do the members of a kibbutz work for themselves?

20 Some words connected with Judaism and the Jews have been hidden in this word box. They might be printed across, upwards or downwards, or diagonally, but always in a straight line. You can use letters more than once. Can you find these ten words:

ARK,
HEBREW,
KOSHER,
MATZA,
PASSOVER,
RABBI,
SHABBAT,
SEDER,
TEMPLE
TORAH?

B	P	A	S	S	O	V	E	R	W
K	O	S	H	E	R	Z	A	A	A
R	C	T	F	D	A	L	T	B	Z
A	B	D	O	E	M	N	R	B	T
Y	H	E	B	R	E	W	S	I	A
S	H	A	B	B	A	T	H	Q	M
R	L	T	V	O	A	H	G	H	J
K	O	Q	T	E	M	P	L	E	R

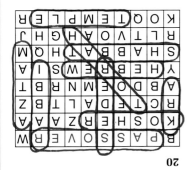

Glossary

Abraham
The founder of the Jewish religion.

Ark
The cupboard in the synagogue where the Scrolls of Torah are kept.

Barmitzvah
Means 'Son of the Commandment'. Ceremony to mark the occasion when a 13 year old boy is accepted as part of the religious community. The same event for 12 year old girls is called Batmitzvah.

Exodus
The journey of the Jews, led by Moses, back to Israel after their slavery in Egypt.

Hannukka
The winter festival of lights.

Hebrew
The language of the Torah and Jewish prayer and the official language of Israel.

Holocaust
The mass murder of Jews ordered by Adolf Hitler during the Second World War.

kibbutz
A community in Israel where people live and work for the good of the kibbutz.

kipah
The small cap worn by Jewish men.

kitel
A white robe worn by Jewish men on special occasions in the synagogue.

kosher
Food that has been prepared according to Jewish law.

Moses
The leader of the Jews, who received God's Ten Commandments on Mount Sinai.

parokhet
The curtain which is drawn across the front of the Ark in the synagogue.

Passover
The spring festival which celebrates the Jews' Exodus from Egypt.

Petikhah
The name given to the ceremony of drawing the curtain in front of the Ark and removing a Scroll of Torah during a service in the synagogue.

Rabbi
The chief official of the synagogue, who is also a teacher and community leader.

Scrolls of Torah
The scrolls which are kept inside the Ark in each synagogue. They contain the words of the Torah.

seder
The family meal held to celebrate Passover.

Shabbat
The Jewish holy day, which lasts from Friday evening until Saturday evening.

shehitah
The slaughter of animals for kosher food.

shiva
The week of mourning after a Jewish person's death.

Simkhat Torah
A festival at the end of Sukkot to give thanks for the Torah.

sukka
The shelter built by Jewish families for Sukkot.

Sukkot
The autumn harvest festival.

synagogue
The Jewish place of worship and community centre.

tallit
A cloak worn by men when praying.

tefillin
Two small leather boxes worn by Jewish men at morning prayer. They contain passages from the Torah.

Torah
The Jewish holy book, which is the first five books of the Bible.

Temple
The building built by King Solomon in Jerusalem, which was the central place of worship for Jews.

Yiddish
A Jewish language based on Hebrew and German.

Yom Kippur
The Day of Atonement. A Holy Day when Jews repent of their sins.

Zionism
The movement dedicated to recreating Israel as the Jewish homeland.

Index